What Happens at a
Zoo?

By Lisa M. Guidone

Reading Consultant: Susan Nations, M.Ed.,
author/literacy coach/consultant in literacy development

WEEKLY READER®
PUBLISHING

Please visit our web site at www.garethstevens.com.
For a free catalog describing Gareth Stevens Publishing's list of high-quality books,
call 1-800-542-2595 (USA) or 1-800-387-3178 (Canada). Our fax: 877-542-2596

Library of Congress Cataloging-in-Publication Data

Guidone, Lisa M.
      What happens at a zoo? / by Lisa M. Guidone.
          p. cm. — (Where people work)
      Includes bibliographical references and index.
      ISBN-10: 0-8368-9272-0   ISBN-13: 978-0-8368-9272-7 (lib. bdg. : alk. paper)
      ISBN-10: 0-8368-9371-9   ISBN-13: 978-0-8368-9371-7 (softcover : alk. paper)
      1. Zoos—Juvenile literature. I. Title.
  QL76.G85   2009
  636.088'9—dc22   2008010818

This edition first published in 2009 by
Weekly Reader® Books
An Imprint of Gareth Stevens Publishing
1 Reader's Digest Road
Pleasantville, NY 10570-7000 USA

Buddy® is a registered trademark of Weekly Reader Corporation. Used under license.

Senior Managing Editor: Lisa M. Herrington
Creative Director: Lisa Donovan
Designer: Alexandria Davis
Photo Coordinator: Charlene Pinckney

Photo credits: Julie Larsen Maher © Wildlife Conservation Society (pages 1, 5, 7, 9, 11, 15, 17, 19, 21);
Dennis DeMello © Wildlife Conservation Society (page 13).

The publisher thanks the Wildlife Conservation Society for its participation in the development of
this book.

Printed in the United States of America

1 2 3 4 5 6 7 8 9 10 09 08

Hi, Kids!

I'm Buddy, your Weekly Reader® pal. Have you ever visited a zoo? I'm here to show and tell what happens at a zoo. So, come on. Turn the page and read along.

Boldface words appear in the glossary.

Welcome to the **zoo**! Many people make up the zoo's crew. A worker greets a mom and her son. He helps them read a map.

map

5

Zookeepers care for the animals. They make sure that the animals are fed and healthy. This zookeeper feeds a giraffe a carrot.

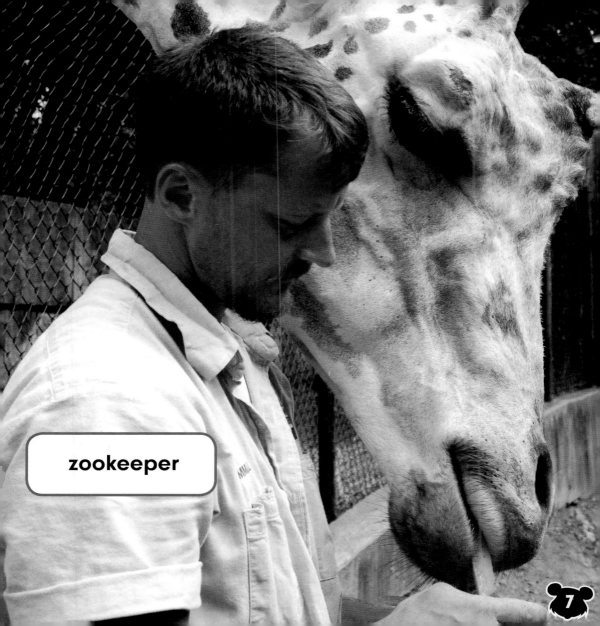

zookeeper

This zookeeper feeds a fish to a sea lion. The sea lion won't chew the fish. It will swallow the whole fish.

Zookeepers have busy jobs. They also clean the places where the animals live.

Zoo animals go to the doctor, just as you do. A **vet** is an animal doctor. This vet gives a red panda a checkup.

vet

13

Vets care for tigers and other wild animals. Look at the tiger's big teeth!

Artists at the zoo design the **exhibits**. An exhibit is an area for people to see where the animals live.

artist

Some zoo workers help animals. Others help people. A **guide** on a train tells a family about the animals.

18

guide

19

People who visit the zoo sometimes get hungry. Workers help with food and snacks. Time for a pretzel before you go!

Glossary

exhibits: areas that are shown to visitors; at a zoo, these areas are where animals live

guide: a person who shows and explains things of interest to people visiting a place, such as a zoo

vet: an animal doctor (short for *veterinarian*)

zoo: a place where animals are kept for people to see and study them

zookeepers: people who work at a zoo and care for the animals

For More Information

Books

I Want to Be a Zookeeper. Dan Liebman (Firefly Books, 2003)

The Zoo. Jacqueline Laks Gorman (Gareth Stevens Publishing, 2005)

Web Sites

Animal Planet: Animals A to Zoo

animal.discovery.com/guides/atoz/atoz.html
Explore the animal world through fun facts, photos, and videos.

Wildlife Conservation Society

www.wcs.org
Find out what is being done to help protect animals.

Publisher's note to educators and parents: Our editors have carefully reviewed these web sites to ensure that they are suitable for children. Many web sites change frequently, however, and we cannot guarantee that a site's future contents will continue to meet our high standards of quality and educational value. Be advised that children should be closely supervised whenever they access the Internet.

Index

About the Author

Lisa M. Guidone works in children's publishing. She has written and edited children's books and magazines for Weekly Reader for nearly eight years. She lives in Trumbull, Connecticut, with her husband, Ryan. She dedicates this book to her new nephew, Anthony, in hopes he shares her love of reading.

Contents

Foreword

BUCKINGHAM PALACE

The United Kingdom Antarctic Heritage Trust aims to ensure that Port Lockroy and the other historic huts on the Antarctic Peninsula survive in the best possible condition for future generations. These fragile structures are part of a unique legacy from Britain's continued scientific endeavour on the continent.

Visiting these huts which still contain all the paraphernalia of day to day living, is a privilege and a poignant experience. The presence of those people who spent so much time together, in such an extreme environment, is still part of the fabric of the buildings; and I believe will remain that way. What they went to do is an extraordinary story in itself and how much they achieved is remarkable. They opened doors for the rest of us to understand so much about the Antarctic continent, and for this we should be eternally grateful.

As Patron of the United Kingdom Antarctic Heritage Trust I urge all who can, and especially the growing numbers of people who have taken the new opportunities to visit Antarctica, to support the Trust in their vital work to safeguard the historic sites in Antarctica.

Anne

Looking into Port Lockroy from Jabet Peak
64°49'S 63°30'W

Fief Mountains

Doumer Island

Jougla Point

Goudier Island

Welcome to Port Lockroy...

... a safe haven for sailors and scientists for more than a hundred years.

Port Lockroy is a sheltered harbour off the coast of Wiencke Island at the meeting of three seaways which offer some of the most dramatic mountain and glacier scenery on the west side of the Antarctic Peninsula. For more than a century Port Lockroy has been a home for explorers, whalers, scientists, and sailors who have made vital contributions to Antarctic history and the harbour has become the most popular visitor destination in Antarctica today.

Base 'A' which stands on Goudier Island in the east of the harbour was the first permanent base to be established on

the Antarctic Peninsula. It was built in February 1944 as part of a wartime mission code-named Operation Tabarin and the building was occupied until January 1962.

In 1996 the British Antarctic Survey, with the assistance of the UK Foreign and Commonwealth Office and UK Antarctic Heritage Trust (UKAHT) restored the base to its original condition. The UKAHT now opens Port Lockroy each summer as a living museum. Proceeds from the gift shop and post office pay for the operation of Port Lockroy and help to safeguard other British historic sites on the continent.

A short history of Port Lockroy

The Belgica

Port Lockroy is one of the few harbours on the Antarctic Peninsula with a secure anchorage. It was discovered in 1873 by Eduard Dallmann, in his steamship *Grönland*, who named the Roosen Strait. The next expedition ship to enter the harbour was the *Belgica* in February 1898. Adrien de Gerlache de Gomery, unaware the channel had already been named, called it the Neumayer Channel: he also named Wiencke Island and Wall Range.

The Français

On 19 February 1904 Jean-Baptiste Charcot, during his French Antarctic Expedition of 1903-5 in his ship the *Français*, needed a safe area to repair his ship's condensers.

On his second expedition four years later, Charcot rough-charted the bay, which he named after expedition supporter Edouard Lockroy, and he named the small rocky island in the east of the bay Goudier Island after the ship's chief mechanic. This was to be the first of many important pieces of survey research carried out at Port Lockroy during the twentieth century. This work was done while he beached his ship the *Porquois-Pas?* in nearby Dorian Bay for repairs to her stem. Charcot's reports of whales were of great interest to the Norwegian whalers based at Deception Island who were in search of new hunting grounds. A pattern for the whaling season developed in which operations started in the South Shetlands and moved down the Antarctic Peninsula as the whales migrated south through the summer.

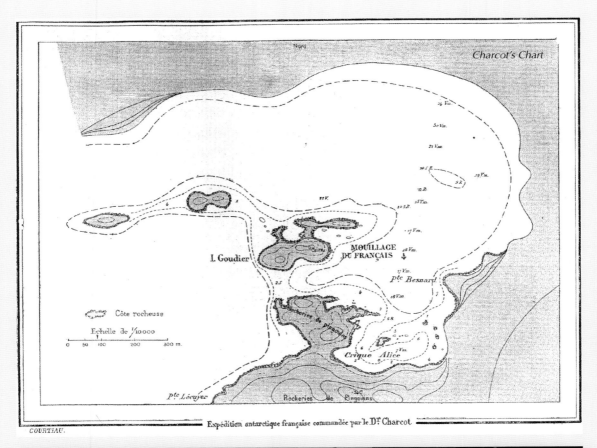

Charcot's Chart

I. Goudier

MOUILLAGE DU FRANÇAIS

Pte Besnard

Côte rocheuse

Echelle de 1/10000

0   50   100   200   300 m.

Crique Alice

Pte Lécuyer

Rockeries de Pingouins

Expédition antarctique française commandée par le Dr Charcot

COURTIAU.

Whale flensing

By 1911 'floating factory' whaling ships were stationed at Port Lockroy. In 12 years of operation 3146 whales were processed here. Whaling companies attempted to claim exclusive 'rights' to good anchorages but in 1920 the Governor of the Falkland Islands required all moorings to be removed unless the whaling companies had express permission to lay them.

The *Penola* at Port Lockroy

On 22 January 1935, the British Graham Land Expedition (BGLE) arrived aboard the schooner *Penola*, led by John Rymill. With just a few members, an aircraft, dogs and two tracked vehicles, it set new standards in meticulous planning, the scope of its scientific programmes and the harmony and care with which its objectives were achieved.

The BGLE bridges the time and geographical gap between the 'heroic age' of Antarctic exploration and the modern era utilising the most successful methods of travel and honing them to lay the foundations for post war operations.

The BGLE Fox Moth at Port Lockroy

Air survey photography and mapping was carried out for 1,000 miles of the Graham Land coast and the expedition set a pattern of living and working in the Antarctic which influenced all the expeditions which followed. All sixteen members of the landing party received the Polar Medal.

During the Second World War the British Government mounted a mission, code-named Operation Tabarin, to establish a permanent presence in Antarctica to assert its territorial claims. Pictured above are the members of the mission while in the tropics on their way South.

Bases were established at Port Lockroy, Deception Island and Hope Bay in order to enhance British sovereignty in the area. Port Lockroy was designated Base 'A'. The largest building on the island is known as 'Bransfield House' after Edward Bransfield, the naval officer in command of the expedition that discovered the Antarctic Peninsula in 1820. It contains the rooms where men stationed at Base 'A' would have worked, eaten and slept. The Boulton & Paul prefabricated 'Spitzbergen' hut now incorporates the bunkroom, radio room and entrance area of the kitchen. The rest of the main building was manufactured from timber brought down from the old whaling station on Deception Island and from the wooden whale factory platforms left by the whalers in Port Lockroy in 1931.

In 1945 the war ended and all British activity in Antarctica was taken on by the Colonial Office (now known as the Foreign and Commonwealth Office). The focus of the work was now to be science and exploration and was renamed the 'Falkland Islands Dependencies Survey' (FIDS).

Under FIDS, scientists at Port Lockroy carried out some of the most important geophysics research as well as work of the modern Antarctic era, studying short wave radio communication, ionospherics, geomagnetism, botany, geology and meteorology.

Base 'A' would be manned permanently (with the exception of three winters) until 1962 when the work moved to more modern research stations elsewhere and Port Lockroy was closed.

When you arrive...

You are likely to land at the rusted mooring chains on Goudier Island.

Mooring points were used by whaling ships during the period 1911-31 and were installed by several ships including the *Solstreif* (pictured above and below), the first 'floating factory' to use Port Lockroy in 1911. Floating factory whaling ships processed whale carcasses by rendering them down to produce oil, bone and meat meal.

Other whaling day relics, including whale bones, can be seen on the lower part of the island near the boatshed. The boat with a flat stern, was used as a floating platform for flensing whale carcasses secured alongside the ship. The other boat, called a 'jolle', which is pointed at both ends, is a water boat for carrying fresh water to the ship from melt streams on the glacier. The Port Lockroy area was a known source of fresh water coming off the nearby glaciers. On the sea bed behind the island are numerous whale bones. There are further whale bones more visible on nearby Jougla Point on Wiencke Island.

During the 1940s and 50s working boats were used by the men for fishing, to reach nearby landmarks and to board visiting ships. Today there are no boats and the boatshed is used for storage.

After 50 years, the anemometer tower has now been re-united with the wind vane and anemometer which once stood at the top of the pole. Because the meteorological conditions at Port Lockroy were so local, they were not actually very useful in building up the wider picture of Peninsula weather.

Mapping has always been key in the work of the British scientists in Antarctica. This map of Goudier Island was hand drawn by Dave Burkitt, one of the 1996 restoration team. It points out the key historical features on the island and can be seen hanging on the corridor wall of Bransfield House.

One or two sledges would have been kept on base for moving stores and the occasional surveying trip to the surrounding area. Dogs were used in 1948 to assist sledging at Port Lockroy – at other times sledges were man-hauled.

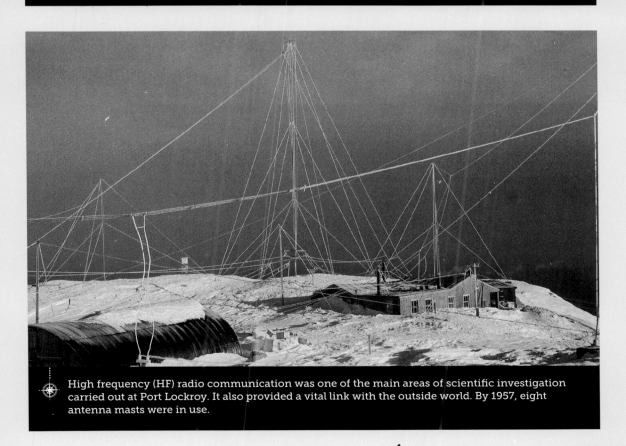

High frequency (HF) radio communication was one of the main areas of scientific investigation carried out at Port Lockroy. It also provided a vital link with the outside world. By 1957, eight antenna masts were in use.

The Nissen Hut

The Nissen hut which was built in 1944 as a storehouse and emergency refuge (see first construction picture right), collapsed during the thirty years when the base was abandoned. The reconstruction (pictured right below) you see today was built in 2010 on the exact site and to the same external Nissen hut specifications but with modern internal insulation, fittings and windows. It provides warm accommodation for the seasonal staff who work at Port Lockroy each summer and is not open to the public.

Until the summer of 2010 staff lived in the old 1947-1961 bunkroom of Bransfield House and used kerosene pressure lamps for lighting. The new Nissen hut provides a fit-for-purpose space and offers privacy. Its innovative adaptation won an award from the British Institute of Structural Engineers.

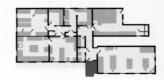

Men would remove their boots in the porch as they came in. It was important not to bring excess snow and water into the building which would make it damp.

Look out for two pairs of skis and snowshoes which were used when travelling over sea ice or snow-covered terrain while on surveying trips.

The black 'Head' skis (in use here and seen hanging on the porch wall) are fitted with a variation of Kandahar bindings with ankle-fitting retaining straps and early 'bear-claw' toe fittings. The skis come with a pair of seal skins (fitted to the skis) and two spare Kandahar heel springs. They belonged to Arthur George Lewis who used them at Port Lockroy in 1959.

There is also an Aldis lamp which was used for signalling by Morse code. While the base was operational, this lamp was located in the porch for easy access and it plugged into a power supply located in the ceiling area near the bathroom door. The socket is still there.

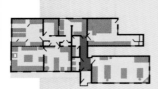

There are a number of interesting objects to see in the hall, including a US Geological Survey aerial photograph.

Look out for the firefighting equipment: two fire extinguishers, breathing apparatus and an instruction card. Fire was always a significant threat in timber framed huts heated by coal stoves.

The original coal bunker can be seen in the wall on the right hand side. This along with coal stored outside would supply the four solid fuel heaters and cooker.

A letter from the British Broadcasting Corporation hangs on the wall at the far end, opposite the front door. It asks for reports and recommendations on the BBC's weekly programme 'Calling the Antarctic', compèred by Peter King, which was commissioned specifically for the FIDS bases. The signature tune, chosen by base members, was 'There is nothing like a Dame' from the musical 'South Pacific'. The programme included record requests, news of the next year's programme and recorded messages from parents, wives and girlfriends. The last item was always hugely entertaining for all listeners although in some cases an embarrassment for the recipient.

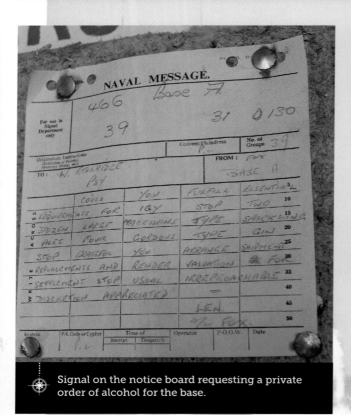

Signal on the notice board requesting a private order of alcohol for the base.

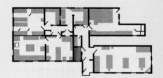

The bathroom is the first room on the left. Taking a bath depended on how many men were on base. Each man took turns to collect snow and ice which was needed for cooking, washing and bathing. Because of the very clean and dry working environment, baths were taken infrequently during winter months. Clean water was readily available as penguins did not begin nesting on the island until 1983, meaning snow drifts were unpolluted: in midsummer, glacier ice was melted when snow was at a minimum.

The meltwater tank was heated by the stove in the living room on the other side of the wall.

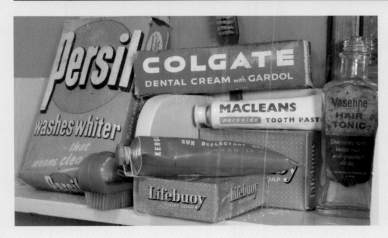

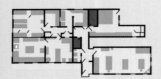

The base leader was responsible for the smooth running of the base and the harmonious relationships of the inhabitants, although it was everyone's responsibility to get on well. Life on a small Antarctic base is egalitarian and the base leader was required to take an equal share of chores.

The pattern of life on base revolved around the annual duty roster, which allocated the weekly cook, also the 'gash hand' who washed dishes, looked after the stoves, emptied the latrine bucket and filled the water tanks. This rota also allocated a room to each member for the routine Saturday cleaning of the hut.

The black and white photo shows Alan Cameron, base leader in 1959, in the office. Until 1957 there was no dedicated office and the base leader had to work at the desk to the right of the fireplace in the Ionospherics room.

James Marr, (pictured below), the overall field commander of Operation Tabarin, was the first base leader at Port Lockroy. He had first ventured to Antarctica as 'Scout Marr' on Shackleton's *Quest* expedition in 1921, and had been a biologist on the *Discovery* Investigations.

The darkroom was set up for developing rolls of 'ionogram' soundings, the primary scientific work. These were analysed on site to provide data for transmission to the Radio Research Station in England. It was also used for recreational photography, and was rebuilt in the workshop after 1958.

Beyond the darkroom is the workshop where base staff built fixtures and fittings and repaired outboard motors, sledges or survey equipment. There is a snatch block for raising heavy weights and a wooden tool box with all its contents. This room also housed the generators but with the scientific need for 24 hour power a new shed was built for three generators. Chippy Ashton, Port Lockroy carpenter in 1944 (pictured above), made ships in bottles adopting the unusual method of inserting the ship bow first.

At the back of the workshop is the latrine, always referred to as the 'heads' (from naval terminology). The gash hand was responsible for emptying the latrine bucket every Saturday into the sea on the west coast of the Island.

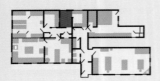

The duty cook was responsible for providing meals and baking bread on the anthracite-fired stove. Snow or ice blocks were brought in from outside and melted in the large copper tank to provide fresh water. Except for the three early winters when there was a permanent cook, each man would take it in turn to produce nourishing meals for the rest of the team. This would very occasionally be supplemented by seal and penguin meat. Base members would collect several hundred penguin eggs from neighbouring islands each year to provide a welcome change to their diet. Only one egg was taken from each nest.

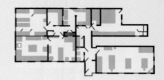

By today's standards the diet on British bases in the 1940s and 50s left something to be desired, but it has to be remembered that food continued to be rationed in Britain for several years after the War. Despite this, all members of the base ate well. In 1945 Mackenzie Lamb commented that their seven-course Christmas dinner was much better than they would get in a restaurant at home. Following a shipping error in 1948, Ken Pawson recalled, '*We were becoming tired of Spam for breakfast. Cocoa was occasionally sweetened with marmalade: we had problems making bread, for there was no yeast*'.

Without a deep-freeze, stores were limited to tinned meat and canned or dried vegetables. But through the cook's ingenuity at replicating '*home cooking*', all the men ate well. The cook was expected to regularly produce fresh bread, cakes and pastries. Powdered egg was adequate for cooking but there were plenty of fresh penguin eggs in season. When cooked, the albumen of a penguin egg does not turn white but remains translucent. With an orange yolk, a boiled or fried penguin egg was not very appealing visually, but it was excellent scrambled or as an omelette.

Tinned meats, such as stewing steak, made acceptable pies and puddings but pre-cooked, shapeless meat becomes monotonous and lacks taste and texture. Fresh meat was occasionally obtained in the form of seal, penguin, shag and occasionally fish. Removing the blubber from seals and birds got rid of the fishy taste and the very dark flesh was palatable to some members. Seal liver was appreciated by some. The items most missed were fresh fruit and vegetables which could not be supplied locally and were a very welcome gift from visiting ships.

Opposite the kitchen you will notice a cupboard in the wall which served as a larder for stowing those foods that would be ruined if frozen, such as tinned fruit and vegetables, tinned kippers, asparagus, beer, evaporated milk and various bottled items such as pickles and sauces. Food not damaged by frost was stored in the Nissen hut, along with a small Stanley cooking stove and emergency radio equipment, in case there was ever a fire in the main building. All of the provisions supplied were either tinned or dried and were shipped down at the beginning of the season to last the men throughout the winter: sufficient stock for 18 months had to be held. A new supply was not delivered until the end of winter when the sea ice was thin enough for a ship to arrive. A varied diet was important and many of the brands on show are still in existence today such as Tate & Lyle sugar, Nestle powdered milk and Quaker porridge oats.

This tank contained hot water for use in the kitchen. This was heated by the Esse cooker, which also heated a radiator in the radio room.

The living room was the social centre of the base and meals were eaten around a large table. One wall was lined with a well stocked library, including magazines. On one occasion a member of another Antarctic base wrote to 'Woman's Own' magazine resulting in a flood of letters - so many that they, along with free magazines, were distributed to all of the Antarctic bases. The letters included one lady who wrote weekly about the activity of her pet parrot.

'Drinks night' was on Saturday, after the weekly clean-up. Men would chat around the bar and records were played on the gramophone. The gramophone you see today is identical to the one which was on base in 1954; this one was donated by the London Gramophone and Phonograph Society. Electronic record players were in use from 1952, but the gramophone was brought out from time to time thereafter to play the old shellac records.

The base was heated with solid fuel stoves and electric heaters and the living room was one of the warmest rooms in the building. The cast iron ['Tortoise'] stove in the far right corner of the room was found under the workshop area during the 1996 restoration of the base. It was removed, cleaned and repainted before being put back in the lounge. The motto reads, 'Slow but sure combustion'. The stove was in use for one year, before being replaced by the much more efficient Esse 'Q' room heater, which was later moved to the bunkroom.

There is a domestic wireless set on the table, and photographs of Queen Elizabeth II and the Duke of Edinburgh on the wall. Photographs of Her Majesty the Queen hung in every British Antarctic base and Port Lockroy was no exception. The British Union flag is still flown at every British base on the continent. The small 'Bonfire' stove in the corner heated water in the bathroom melt tank.

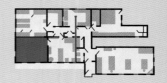

The ionospherics room was used to house meteorological and ionospheric equipment. It provided a place to carry out scientific investigations which are explained further overleaf.

In the middle of the room stands the Union Radio Mark II Ionosonde. Delivered to Port Lockroy in 1953, this was one of the most important pieces of machinery at Port Lockroy and the one you see today is identical to the one which would have been here originally. It was nicknamed 'The Beastie' due to its size and weight, complexity, and its interference with radio and gramophone. The ionosphericists who analysed the results of the ionograms were known as 'Beastiemen'. This particular machine was made in 1959 and acquired and restored in 2001 by Alan Carroll, base leader at Port Lockroy from 1954-57, and shipped to Port Lockroy the following year.

Before the base had a dedicated office, the ionospherics and other communal spaces were used for administrative tasks.

There is a Navy B28 shortwave radio receiver in the room which was the standard receiver used at Port Lockroy when the base was operational. This was used for receiving time-standard signals and setting the timing on the whistler tape recorder. Other pieces of equipment are displayed around the walls: a barograph, a thermograph, a hydrograph, an anemometer, a wooden whirling psychrometer and test tubes.

Ionospherics

The ionosphere (a region of the upper atmosphere above approx 100km) reflects or absorbs radio waves depending on the frequency of the waves; reflection of high-frequency radio waves by the ionosphere was the chief means of long distance communication before satellites. The primary work undertaken at Port Lockroy focussed on measurement of the varying density and height of this reflective layer above the station.

Similar to radar, pulses were transmitted into the atmosphere and reflected off the various layers of the ionosphere. Their echoes were received and recorded as ionograms on 30m reels of photographic paper which were developed in Port Lockroy's tiny darkroom. This information was vital in forecasting the best frequency to use in long range radio communication as well as being crucial to the discovery of a global wind system in the upper atmosphere over the Antarctic Peninsula.
The station formed part of a global network of similar observatories, work that continues today with the ionospheric soundings being carried out by the British Antarctic Survey from Halley and Rothera. It was study of the long-term ionospheric data from Base 'A' and later from farther south at British base 'F' Faraday, that led to the discovery of the hole in the ozone layer.

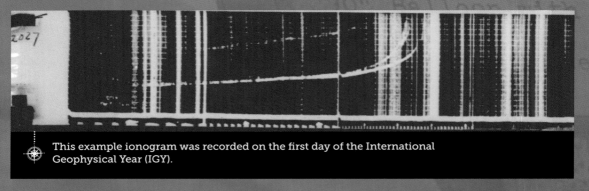

This example ionogram was recorded on the first day of the International Geophysical Year (IGY).

Whistlers

Although ionospheric soundings were the mainstay of research at Port Lockroy a separate set of data was collected about 'whistlers'. 'Whistlers' are the product of low frequency electro-magnetic pulses generated by lightning strikes. These travel into space along the Earth's magnetic field to ultimately return to Earth in the opposite hemisphere. As a pulse crosses the equator it can be as much as 40,000 km out in space. A receiver in the hemisphere where the lightning-strike occurs will receive these as a 'click' while in the opposite hemisphere it arrives as a 'swish' or a descending whistle, caused by the higher frequencies travelling faster than the lower ones (hence the name). The scientific interest is in the delay in the arrival of the whistler, and in its spectral signature which together provide information about the atomic particle population in space above the equator. Whistlers were recorded from 1957 onwards as part of the International Geophysical Year (IGY). In 1958 it was suggested that transmissions of a similar frequency range to whistlers could be received by deeply submerged submarines without compromising their 'stealth ability'. As a result a small test transmitter was set up in the USA to send coded signals that would arrive in the vicinity of the Antarctic Peninsula, and in 1959 a prototype receiver was sent to Port Lockroy to monitor and report them. After much development a final system 'Project ELF' was able to transmit extremely powerful signals that would spread across the world and be received at great depths in order to authorise Intercontinental Ballistic Missile (ICBM) action by individual submarines, bringing about a stalemate in the Cold War. The American system was not closed until the 21st Century, after alternative warning systems were developed. Routine scientific study of whistlers continues at various Antarctic bases.

Meteorology

The scientific work on the Antarctic Peninsula was largely financed by a tax on whale oil so an important function of the bases was to provide data for weather forecasts for the whaling fleets. Synoptic weather reporting was the first programme to commence at Base 'A'. At first only barometric pressure, air temperature, and relative humidity were recorded, but an anemometer was later rigged on top of a 10m mast to record wind speed. A sunshine recorder and rain gauge followed. Thermometers and thermographs were kept in a Stevenson screen (it is still on top of the island but another example can be seen in the Ionospherics room). The duty 'met man' had to brave all weathers and read the instruments every three hours. Regular observations at Port Lockroy ceased after 1952 however, because the bay was found far from an ideal place for a meteorological reporting station. It is subject to localised atmospheric conditions that do not accurately reflect the neighbourhood's weather.

In addition, pilot balloons were tracked by theodolite to calculate wind speed and direction at different altitudes.

To ensure a constant rate of ascent (500 feet per minute was standard at that time) the balloon was first slightly over-filled with hydrogen, using the Balloon Filler (with the weight appropriate to its diameter) attached to the neck of the balloon. The valve on the filler was then used to release surplus hydrogen until the balloon was neither sinking nor rising. The filler (including the weight) was then removed and the neck of the balloon was tied off. This meant that the balloon was now 'lighter than air' and ready to be released. A theodolite reading was taken at sixty-second intervals to record the height of the balloon and its direction from the point of release. The record height was 23,317 metres.

All the men at Port Lockroy shared one bedroom and each bunk was supplied with mattresses, pillows, sheets and blankets. With no personal space available it was understood by all that a man's bunk was the equivalent of his private bedroom. From 1952 it was heated by an electric convector heater later replaced by an Esse solid fuel heater, still in position.

Whilst converting the bunkroom back to its original appearance, murals were discovered on the walls of each bunk. These were painted in 1960 by Evan Watson the diesel mechanic who also painted the mural of Marilyn Monroe on the back of the generator shed door. Each bunk is adorned with a carefully hand-painted picture of a star of the Hollywood silver screen including Diana Dors, Ava Gardner, Elizabeth Taylor, Doris Day, Jayne Mansfield, Sophia Loren and Jane Russell. These murals were painted over in the 1980s while the base was abandoned and it is still a mystery as to who covered them up and why.

The last flag flown at the base can be seen on the far wall, along with some personal possessions and items of clothing. A field ration box is displayed, with a knife and a compass which would have been used on field trips. A cloth badge reading 'Antarctic Ski Club' is displayed on the sleeve of a coat; the Antarctic ski club was a member-only club amongst the men of Port Lockroy with its own set of rules.

The radio operator was an important man on base because the radio provided a vital link with the outside world. On an Antarctic base friends and family seem very far away and contact is important. To begin with, all official messages had to be encrypted – a tedious but exacting job – but after three months security relaxed sufficiently for weather details to be sent in international code, but all other messages had to be sent in ciphered form until the end of World War II in Europe.

In winter, men could send a monthly 100-word radio message to their next of kin and receive 200 words. Outgoing messages were transmitted by Morse code to Stanley in the Falkland Islands, typed onto airmail forms and despatched to the UK with ordinary mail. It wasn't much, but it enabled men to keep in touch with their families. The Morse key can be seen on the desk. During the war, men at Port Lockroy had a poignant reminder of life at home when they could hear anti-aircraft guns firing as the chimes of Big Ben died away before the nine o'clock news. The Queen's speech was always listened to over the BBC World Service on Christmas Day. Look out for the 1944 typewriter, clandestine transmitter, rotary converter, field radio, radio receiver and its control box and frequency meter.

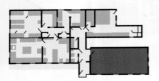

The Enfield generator, one of many which were made and supplied by Auto Diesels Ltd in Uxbridge, UK, still sits in the middle of the room. It provided backup power in case of breakdowns. Manhandling the many drums of fuel required by the generators from the landing point to the rear of the hut each summer was an arduous and dangerous task! From 1957, the generator was run to power an electric pump to deliver fuel from the beach to a bulk storage tank behind Bransfield House.

Pictured below are the generators being hauled up from the landing site and being installed.

Evan Watson was the diesel mechanic on base in 1960 and painted the life-size mural of Marilyn Monroe on the back of the door. You can see his initials 'EW'.

Life at Lockroy

Survey work

Port Lockroy was rated as a 'static scientific base' rather than a 'sledging base' but short expeditions were made to Wiencke, Anvers and Doumer Islands. Surveys were made using a plane-table, rangefinder and panoramic camera. Compass bearings were also taken of prominent features along the mainland coast and on distant islands which could not be reached.

Geological and biological specimens were collected and one party even experimented with burning lichens growing on rocks as an emergency fuel! Sledges were used for these short journeys, with a bicycle wheel attached to the back of the sledge to measure the distance between two survey points.

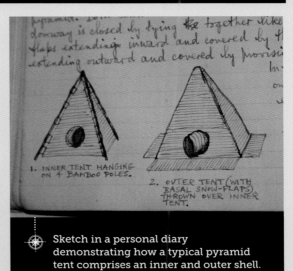

Sketch in a personal diary demonstrating how a typical pyramid tent comprises an inner and outer shell.

Survey work varied considerably depending on weather conditions, resources available and the aims of the survey being undertaken.

In 1944 the bad weather permitted survey work on only one day in four. The rest of the time was spent in sleeping bags. Unless there was good sea-ice, journeys from Port Lockroy started with a boat journey from Goudier Island to Doumer, Wiencke or Anvers Islands. Most journeys from Port Lockroy were made by man-hauling sledges. In 1948, two husky dogs arrived at Port Lockroy. Although they were more pets than working dogs, 'Pretty' and 'Peter' were used for extra pulling power to help the men hauling a heavy sledge. A short series of soundings around the back of the bay was made from an unpowered dinghy. It was described as

'uncomfortable and occasionally dangerous'. The soundings close to glaciers were therefore reduced to a very few, owing to pieces of ice frequently breaking off. A Royal Navy team made a detailed hydrographic survey of the approaches to Port Lockroy in 1956 and accurately positioned submerged rocks and small islands. There was considerable secrecy about the Navy team's arrival at Port Lockroy. This turned out to be because they were checking anchorages for the Royal Yacht *Britannia* carrying HRH Prince Philip on a tour of the British bases.

One sledging party had a narrow escape: "*We heard a deafening roar like the crackling of continuous thunder and glancing up saw a great mass of ice break away and come hurtling down on us. We threw ourselves flat on our stomachs hands over heads (instinctively I think) in a forlorn effort to protect them. We had scarcely got into this position when we were enveloped in the whirling snow cloud so dense that it blotted out the light. ... It was all over in a second or two. The rush of air ceased, the roaring died away, the light returned through the thinning snow cloud and we got to our feet shaken but undamaged. The avalanche had evidently just failed to reach us*".

The Royal Visit

In 1957 HRH The Duke of Edinburgh had been to Australia to inaugurate the Olympic Games in Melbourne and was visiting some of the FIDS bases including Port Lockroy on his return journey to the UK. The Royal Yacht *Britannia* was accompanied by the Navy's ice patrol ship HMS *Protector*. The arrival of the naval survey party in 1956 was unexpected and Bransfield House became overcrowded until the survey team erected their own prefabricated hut, affectionately named The *Sealskin Arms* which was later taken to Jougla Point to act as a maintenance/refuge hut for men working on the remote whistler antenna and receiver.

Wintering

Visitors to Port Lockroy were few and far between at the best of times. Ships with mail, stores and relief personnel visited infrequently during the Antarctic summer (November to April) and in winter the base at Port Lockroy became home to a small and very isolated community of men. Once the ships had left for the UK, the bases were completely cut off throughout the long dark winter.

The normal term of duty in the Antarctic was two winters which meant that men would be away from home for over two and half years. They often moved to another base for the second winter.

One advantage of this length of stay was that there would always be a nucleus of experienced men to provide continuity.

Midwinter's Day is the most important date in the Antarctic calendar. It marks the mid-way point through winter and heralds longer days. Traditionally, a dinner is held on all Antarctic bases to mark the occasion; menus were laboriously drawn and typed as mementoes of an Antarctic winter season.

Medical Matters

During the winter there was no chance of relief by ship or plane and, even in the summer months, pack ice could prevent access to the base. That the men were young and fit reduced the chances of medical problems but there was always the possibility of unexpected illness or accident. Only in the first winter of 1944 did Port Lockroy have a doctor.

The usual procedure was that the base leader was medical officer by default. He had a naval destroyer's medical kit and a copy of the Ship's Captain's Medical Guide. If necessary, radio contact could be made with a doctor. In 1958 one man developed an abscess on a tooth which was extracted with guidance over the radio from a doctor on a nearby base. A mixture of whisky and cocaine pads induced a level of anaesthesia and a tooth was extracted after considerable exertion.

Communications

The only contact with the outside world during winter was wireless telegraphy, using Morse code, with the FIDS office in Stanley, Falkland Islands, or wireless telephony when on the amateur bands.

However, an official post office had been established at each British base when it was built to strengthen the UK's sovereign claim to the territory.

The post office at Port Lockroy opened on 23 March 1944. The first stamps to be used were Falkland Island stamps which were overprinted with 'Graham Land Dependency Of' and men on base would send home packages with a variety of stamps as collectors' items. They are now highly prized. All outgoing mail during World War II was censored. Mail would arrive on relief ships and its delivery had a significant effect on the team's wellbeing. When one ship cancelled its last visit of the season, in April, the base diary recorded: '*No mail and no prospect of any 'til November at the earliest has been the heaviest blow to morale*'.

Pets

Pets were often a part of daily base life at Port Lockroy and at other Antarctic bases. In 1944 when Lockroy was established, a pig was sent down as fresh meat and it lived in a sty made from a wooden crate filled with wood wool. When it was time for her to be used to feed the men, 'Taff' Davies, a Welshman on base at the time, gave her a good meal and, when she had fallen asleep, despatched her with a revolver. He refused to eat the meat as '*it would be like eating one of the family*'.

Dizzy

Eddie & Peso

Several working sledge dogs were 'retired' to Port Lockroy but pets were frequent and much-loved members of the base. This was commonplace on Antarctic bases until a ban on domestic animals was imposed in 1994 under Antarctic Treaty regulations. Favourite pets at Port Lockroy were 'Dizzy' the cat and 'Peso' who had been bought as a puppy in Montevideo. Her name reputedly reflected her price and she liked to go for trips in the dinghy.

The 1946 tsunami

On 2 April 1946 the sea suddenly ebbed away, exposing the seabed between Goudier and Doumer Islands. The men realised that, if the sea returned as fast as it had gone away, the base might be flooded. So they climbed onto the roof of the Nissen hut. When the sea returned, it rose one metre above the high tide mark and washed away one of the three small wooden whaling boats. The men blamed the wave on an iceberg rolling over, but on the previous day a tsunami had been generated off the Aleutian Islands. It caused widespread havoc as it spread down the Pacific. In the Argentine Islands farther south, the old British Graham Land Expedition hut (pictured right) was completely destroyed by a wave whose height was accentuated by the constricted channel through which it came.

Modern tide recorders or Sea Level Recorders are located at several research stations along the Antarctic Peninsula. Their records are used in the determination of the flow of the Antarctic Circumpolar Current and long-term changes in sea level.

www.ukaht.org

31

Aviation

Aerial exploration in Antarctica began remarkably early. The first flight was made in 1928 from Deception Island by Australian Antarctic aviation pioneer Sir Hubert Wilkins, who returned to the Peninsula one year later and flew in his Lockheed Vega from Port Lockroy to Evans Inlet on the east coast at an altitude of 3,000 metres. On subsequent flights he mapped the west coast of the Peninsula from Port Lockroy northwards. Wilkins, like the British Graham Land Expedition after him in 1935, used sea planes and took off on water.

Port Lockroy was used briefly by two more expeditions before the outbreak of World War II. In 1934 Lincoln Ellsworth, having failed to find a suitable airstrip site on Deception Island, visited Port Lockroy, looking for a suitable ice-strip. He failed to find one but was able to take off from Snow Hill Island to cross the continent in the following year. In 1935 the British Graham Land Expedition undertook extensive survey on the Antarctic Peninsula (see page 6).

In the 1970s the glacier opposite Port Lockroy was deemed safe to land a Twin Otter aircraft. A 400 metre ski-way was marked out along the spine of the glacier. Damoy hut in Dorian Bay was erected in 1973. It was used as a summer air facility and transit station with personnel and stores arriving by ship and then flown to Rothera Research Station further south to ensure that the science programmes could start as early in the season as possible.

International Geophysical Year 1957-58

Much of the scientific work carried out at Port Lockroy contributed to the International Geophysical Year (IGY) of 1957-59. This was an 18-month period of coordinated activity and was the first substantial multi-nation research programme in Antarctica. Scientists from 67 countries were involved in the project and data was contributed from 52 stations operating in Antarctica, forming the foundations of the Antarctic Treaty. Port Lockroy acted as the communications centre for the eleven British bases during the IGY as well as undertaking atmospheric research.

The purpose of the IGY was to be '...all embracing, to fit the Earth into the pattern of the universe, to relate its parts together, to discover hidden order and to interpret the whole in relation to space and especially to ... the Sun' (Professor J Wilson).

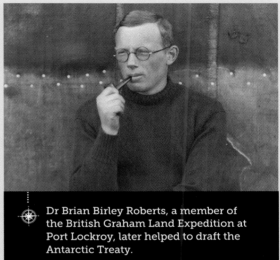

Dr Brian Birley Roberts, a member of the British Graham Land Expedition at Port Lockroy, later helped to draft the Antarctic Treaty.

Closure of Base 'A'

By the 1960s the British Antarctic science programme had moved to more modern research stations elsewhere on the continent and Port Lockroy was no longer deemed necessary. The ionospherics programme was transferred to Base 'F' in the Argentine Islands, 25 miles to the South (now the Ukrainian station Vernadsky). On 16 January 1962, the base was closed down and much of the equipment was transferred, leaving it as an emergency refuge. The base would lie empty and abandoned for the next thirty years.

Yachts exploring the Antarctic Peninsula would occasionally use Port Lockroy as a safe anchorage and cruise ships landing their passengers at Jougla Point would enter the building from time to time. But during this period Bransfield House and the other buildings on Goudier Island began to deteriorate and they eventually became hazardous.

In 1994 a decision was made to clean-up abandoned British bases on the Antarctic Peninsula and determine which should be removed and which could be saved. The Environmental Protocol of the Antarctic Treaty requires that any abandoned building should be removed unless designated a Historic Site or Monument (HSM). The British Antarctic Survey, on behalf of the British Government and UK Antarctic Heritage Trust, carried out a conservation survey and recommended that Port Lockroy be saved due to its importance as a surviving base from Operation Tabarin. Port Lockroy was one of five abandoned bases which were declared HSMs, along with bases 'B', 'E', 'F', and 'Y' ; the remaining abandoned bases were either passed on to other nations or removed. Subsequently Base 'W' and Damoy hut were given historic status. (See page 48 for more information on these bases).

In 1996 a team of carpenters and conservators travelled to Bransfield House to repair the structure of the building and return the interior to its original 1962 condition. The men found the base full of snow and ice and there were penguins nesting in the living room.

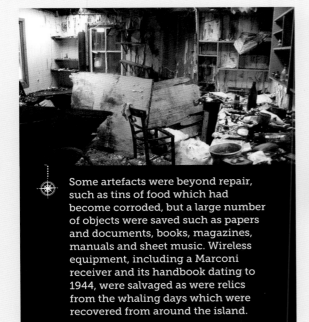

Some artefacts were beyond repair, such as tins of food which had become corroded, but a large number of objects were saved such as papers and documents, books, magazines, manuals and sheet music. Wireless equipment, including a Marconi receiver and its handbook dating to 1944, were salvaged as were relics from the whaling days which were recovered from around the island.

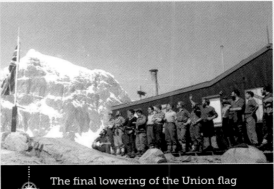

The final lowering of the Union flag when the base was closed in 1962.

Port Lockroy today

Today, Bransfield House exists as a 'living museum'. It is no longer a research station but instead gives a sense of what life was like for the scientists who lived and worked on the first permanent British science base in Antarctica.

The site is cared for by the UK Antarctic Heritage Trust, a British based charity established in 1993, which works to conserve Antarctic buildings and artefacts and to promote and encourage the public's interest in its Antarctic heritage. The Trust was established as a charity in 1993 and Port Lockroy is the Trust's flagship project.

Port Lockroy operates from early November to mid-March every year and is now the busiest landing site on the Antarctic Peninsula. More than 18,000 visitors of all nationalities pass through the doors of the base every summer, arriving on tour ships, yachts, hydrographic ice-breakers and naval patrol vessels.

The base is staffed by a team of four recruits who are seasonally employed by the UKAHT. They live in private quarters in the Nissen Hut and are responsible for the day-to-day running of the museum, post office and shop. Proceeds from the shop are re-invested into the conservation of Port Lockroy and other historic sites on the Peninsula.

The team carries out annual maintenance on Goudier Island to ensure all the structures and artefacts survive through the bleak and blustery winter months. They also help to communicate Port Lockroy's story to visitors and the international media.

The selling of gifts (including original watercolours of gentoo penguins by our artist Una Hurst who has contributed to many of our designs) funds the bulk of our conservation work.

The Post Office

The post office reopened after Bransfield House was restored as a museum in 1996. It is an official post office of the Government of the British Antarctic Territory (GBAT) and is the most southerly public post office in the world. GBAT donates a proportion of the post office revenue to the UKAHT to support our charitable work. Around 70,000 postcards are posted each year to over 100 countries.

All mail posted at Port Lockroy is cancelled by hand and then put on the next ship travelling to the Falkland Islands where it is received by the British Post Office in Stanley, flown to the UK and sent on to its final destination. Mail usually takes 6-8 weeks to arrive.

An official postmark from Port Lockroy is much coveted by stamp collectors and the post office continues to receive considerable philatelic interest from all over the world.

Wildlife

The Antarctic Peninsula region is rich in wildlife and the most biologically diverse area of the Antarctic continent.

Port Lockroy is home to several species of bird and receives frequent visits from a number of Antarctic mammals. Sheathbills (pictured below) - small white birds about the size of a pigeon - nest underneath the front door of Bransfield House. They will steal any penguin egg which is not carefully guarded and have also been known to steal personal possessions such as sunglasses, gloves and socks!

Skuas (pictured below right) and giant petrels also visit the island from time to time, especially when penguin chicks are small and vulnerable. Both birds will steal young chicks without hesitation. In earlier years, before gentoos started to nest at Port Lockroy, kelp gulls were very common: evidence for this were the huge numbers of limpet shells dropped there after being eaten - enough to pave the pathway from the boatshed landing to the base hut.

On 'Bills Island' behind the boatshed there are nesting Antarctic terns and skuas, and there are several hundred pairs of blue-eyed shags at Jougla Point. Snow petrels often make appearances as they flit across the island.
It is not uncommon for seals to come ashore at Port Lockroy, including Weddell seals and fur seals. Leopard seals often patrol the surrounding waters and both minke whales and orcas have been seen in the back bay.

Penguins

In 1908, Louis Gain, an ornithologist on Charcot's French expedition, ringed 50 gentoos at Port Lockroy with coloured plastic rings. He found two during a brief visit the following year and Norwegian whalers later found some ringed birds in 1911. (They ate the birds and sent the rings to France.) Gain's survey showed gentoo penguins nesting on Jougla Point and Adélies nesting on Lecuyer Point (but no penguins were nesting on Goudier Island). This was the first bird-ringing programme in Antarctica and it proved that penguins return to nest in the same place from year to year.

Gentoo penguins first started to nest on Goudier Island in 1983. There are now around 700 breeding pairs. Numbers fluctuate naturally from year to year, but on average each pair will raise two chicks per season and, over their 15-year average lifespan, they produce enough offspring to maintain a stable population.

Port Lockroy is the most visited site in Antarctica and this makes it an ideal place to study whether there is any effect of human tourism on penguin colonies. A monitoring programme has been carried out since the base reopened in 1996 and UK Antarctic Heritage Trust staff continue this important work each year. Half the island is open to tourists and the remaining half is off-limits, reserved as a 'control colony'. The difference in breeding success between the two areas is compared and recorded each year.

Staff at Port Lockroy carry out whole-island counts at four stages during the gentoo breeding cycle; counting the number of nests on the island, the number of eggs laid, the number of chicks which hatch and the number of chicks which 'creche' once they have left the nest. To date, no significant impact from human activity on the island has been detected and the penguin population continues to remain stable.

Adélie and chinstrap penguins do not nest at Port Lockroy although young birds from each species, which wander widely before settling, are regular visitors. Some spend about three weeks ashore while they moult their feathers. Adélie, macaroni and king penguins have also been seen at Port Lockroy and, very occasionally, a solitary Emperor.

Marine Life

Goudier Island is unusual in Antarctica for having a broad expanse of rocky beach at low tide. This makes it easy to study the contents of rock pools and collect specimens. Spiny plunder-fish live under rocks in shallow water and become trapped in rock pools at low tide. Limpets colonise the shore after the sea-ice has dispersed and are a favourite food of kelp gulls.

The UK Antarctic Heritage Trust adheres to the Convention on the Conservation of Antarctic Marine Living Resources (CCAMLR), an ecosystem monitoring and regulation convention which tracks the effects of fishing and the harvesting of species in the area. Once a month at low tide staff at Port Lockroy carry out a beachcombing exercise to identify any manmade items which have been washed onto the island. Any that are found are measured and weighed and the data are submitted. To date nothing of any significance has been found.

Alongside ionospheric research, there was a small scientific programme in 1944 that reflected the interests of the men on base. Botanist Ivan Mackenzie Lamb studied Antarctic lichens and made a terrace garden with soil shipped from the Falkland Islands. Seven species of Falkland flowering plants and ferns were planted and some grew for a while; dandelions and thrift lasted longest.
In 1945, G. 'Jack' Lockley collected many bird and marine samples.

Britain's Antarctic story and the United Kingdom Antarctic Heritage Trust

Antarctica remains the only continent on Earth where humans' first buildings still stand. The UK Antarctic Heritage Trust was established in 1993 to help care for these fragile buildings on behalf of the international community.

Most of Antarctica's historic heritage is British and this is indicative of Britain's long and distinguished involvement on the Antarctic continent since the eighteenth century.

Captain James Cook 1728-1779
RESOLUTION
British Antarctic Territory 55p

Captain James Cook was the first person to cross the Antarctic Circle during his circumnavigation of the Antarctic in 1772-75. Although he did not actually sight the continent, he predicted a "country doomed by Nature to lie buried under everlasting ice and snow".

Sir James Clark Ross 1800 - 1862
EREBUS AND TERROR
British Antarctic Territory 2p

James Weddell 1787 - 1834
JANE AND BEAUFOY
British Antarctic Territory 1p

Two other distinguished British explorers were Captain James Weddell who in 1822 reached 74°15'S and Captain James Clark Ross who in a voyage from 1839 to 1843 discovered the coast of Victoria Land, sighted Mount Erebus and found the continent's largest ice shelf. The Weddell and Ross Seas are named after them.

Edward Bransfield (1820-21) discovered the Antarctic Peninsula; Henry Foster (1929-31) surveyed coasts and ocean currents around the South Shetlands and used a Kater invariable pendulum to make observations on gravity; and John Biscoe (1830-32) made the first sightings of Graham Land and Enderby Land as well as a number of Peninsula islands.

Dr William Spiers Bruce 1867 - 1921
SCOTIA
British Antarctic Territory 65p

William Speirs Bruce led the Scottish National Antarctic Expedition from 1902-4 which discovered Coats Land, established the first manned meteorological station in Antarctica on Laurie Island at the South Orkneys and gathered a collection of biological and geological specimens.

Scott, Shackleton and the 'heroic' age

Cape Adare

Among the continent's most famous heroes are Captain Robert Falcon Scott and Sir Ernest Shackleton who are associated with the 'heroic era' of Antarctic exploration. It was Carsten Borchgrevink however who heralded this epoch with his British Antarctic Expedition of 1898-1900. They spent the first winter on Antarctica and set a record for the most southern point reached. His hut at Cape Adare is the first human structure to be built on the continent.

Hut Point

Scott led two major expeditions to the Ross Sea. The first of these, the National Antarctic Expedition (1901-4 aboard *Discovery*) was a major undertaking which built a base hut at Hut Point, achieved the first ascent to the Polar Plateau and a record traverse south by Scott, Shackleton and Edward Wilson.

Cape Royds

In the interim, Shackleton led his own expedition to Antarctica, 1907-09, with the goal of conquering the South Pole and carrying out a scientific programme. Achieving extraordinary progress, on half rations, Shackleton, Frank Wild, Eric Marshall and Jameson Adams reached within 97 nautical miles of the South Pole. A decision was made to abandon the attempt for fear of running out of supplies and the men returned alive to their hut at Cape Royds. Other notable achievements included the first ascent of Mount Erebus, the discovery of the Beardmore Glacier and a 1,260 mile return journey to the South Magnetic Pole.

Cape Evans

Scott then returned to Antarctica for his second expedition (the British Antarctic Expedition of 1910-13) aboard the *Terra Nova,* building a new hut at Cape Evans. The aim of conquering the South Pole was a firmly fixed objective.

The 'Pole Party' included Edward Wilson, Captain Lawrence Oates, Lt Bowers and Petty Officer Edgar Evans. A treacherous journey South ended on 17 January 1912 when the men reached the Pole only to find that Roald Amundsen's Norwegian expedition had reached the spot 35 days earlier. Scott's journal records that the return journey would be a 'desperate struggle' as the exhausted and demoralised men headed north with a shortage of food and fuel. An injury to Evans' hand did not heal and, following a fall, he became delirious and died on 17 February.

A month later, Captain Oates who by now was debilitated by frostbite, hoped he could relieve pressure on supplies and give the others some hope of returning alive; with the words 'I am just going outside and may be some time" he left the tent and walked to his death in a blizzard. From 21 March, a blizzard trapped the three survivors, Scott, Wilson and Bowers, in their tent only eleven miles from One Ton Depot where rations were waiting. Scott knew they would not make it. His 'Message to the Public' described the hardship of the journey and wrote that '*Had we lived I should have had a tale to tell of the hardihood, endurance and courage of my companions that would have stirred the heart of every Englishman. These rough notes and our dead bodies must tell the tale...*'.

With the South Pole now reached by Amundsen, Shackleton perceived a crossing of the continent from sea to sea as "the one great main objective of Antarctic journeyings" and set about seeking support for the Imperial Trans-Antarctic Expedition (1914-17). The expedition would not achieve its aim but has instead become recognised as an epic feat of human survival when his ship the *Endurance* (left) sank, leaving the men to make their way over the ice and sea to winter on Elephant Island and for Shackleton to make the famous open boat journey to South Georgia.

During 1911-14 British born Douglas Mawson led the Australasian Antarctic Expedition which claimed land for the British Crown (King George V Land and Queen Mary Land) and three wintering parties undertook extensive exploration and scientific research, discovering the first meteorite in Antarctica a few kilometres west of Cape Denison. Most famous is Mawson's epic solo journey to safety after the loss of his two companions.

The Legacy

The huts left behind from these heroic expeditions still survive today. They represent man's first attempts to establish a toehold, even temporarily, on the brutally inhospitable Antarctic continent and are an exceptional physical legacy for the world. The sites in the Ross Sea are cared for by the UK Antarctic Heritage Trust's sister charity, the New Zealand Antarctic Heritage Trust.

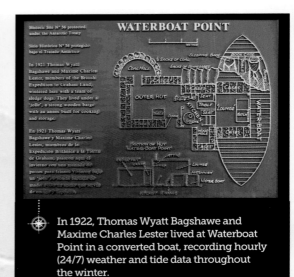

The heroic age of polar exploration, in particular Captain Scott (pictured above at Cape Evans in 1911), inspired future British Antarctic activity: Bagshawe and Lester and the British Graham Land Expedition (BGLE) are viewed as the transition between the heroic age and modern day. Many of the methods from the earlier expeditions were honed and perfected by the BGLE.

In 1922, Thomas Wyatt Bagshawe and Maxime Charles Lester lived at Waterboat Point in a converted boat, recording hourly (24/7) weather and tide data throughout the winter.

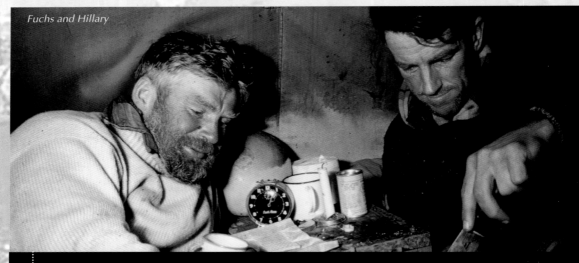

Fuchs and Hillary

During the International Geophysical Year 1957-59, besides the increased scientific activities of the Falkland Islands Dependencies Survey (FIDS), Sir Vivian Fuchs and supported by Sir Edmund Hillary led the Commonwealth Trans-Antarctic Expedition making the first crossing of the Antarctic continent. They became the first expedition to reach the South Pole overland since Amundsen and Scott 46 years earlier.

Joining FIDS in 1947 and spending three consecutive winters at Stonington base, Fuchs was instrumental in shaping the work of FIDS (renamed British Antarctic Survey (BAS) in 1962). It was during the International Geophysical Year that the number of British operational bases on the Antarctic Peninsula was at its height, numbering 11. In all 24 bases were constructed from 1944 to the present day. However, with improvements in logistical capacity and science being concentrated into large, modern research stations many of these older bases outgrew their operational use and were abandoned. In 1994 with the introduction of the Environmental Protocol to the Antarctic Treaty, many of these bases were either handed over to other national research operators or removed. Some, considered important in recognising the scientific and human heritage of Antarctica, were designated as 'historic sites'.

Eight more bases to explore... hundreds of stories to discover

The UK Antarctic Heritage Trust watches over Historic Sites and Monuments on the Antarctic Peninsula.

Deception   62°59'S 60°34'W

 Base 'B' at Deception Island (HSM no 71) was established as part of the wartime Operation Tabarin, occupying the abandoned Hektor whaling station. It acted as the centre for the Falkland Islands Dependencies Aerial Survey Expedition from 1955-57. It was abandoned after it was destroyed by ash flows during the eruption at Deception Island in 1967 and is now an Antarctic Specially Protected Area (ASPA) managed by several nations.

Reclus hut

(carefully dismantled in 1996 and re-erected with its artefacts in the Falkland Islands Museum)

 Reclus Hut, also known as Portal Point, was built in 1956 on an exposed area of rock close to the sea on the tip of Cape Reclus. In 1957, three men from Danco Island (Base 'O') wintered in the small hut in order to carry out local survey work. During the same winter, a team of four men from Hope Bay (Base 'D'), including the famous polar explorer Sir Wally Herbert, set out on an epic sledge journey with two teams of dogs to make the first North-South traverse of the Antarctic Peninsula; the team from the Reclus Hut laid depots for the sledging team and looked for a suitable route for them. The Hope Bay team made the journey to Reclus Hut in 54 days.

Damoy 64°49'S 63°31'W

Damoy Refuge (HSM no 84) lies in Dorian Bay on Wiencke Island. It was originally built as a summer air facility with a ski-way close by. It was intermittently occupied from 1973 to 1993 providing a transit station for those personnel and stores which had arrived by ship to be flown on to Rothera Research Station in early summer when sea ice prevented direct access to the station by sea. This hut represents the pre-modern era of Antarctic science and logistics. Damoy Hut is managed by the UKAHT and each year Port Lockroy seasonal staff visit the hut to carry out general upkeep and maintenance tasks.

Wordie House 65°15'S 64°16'W

Wordie House Base 'F' (HSM no 62) on Winter Island is of historic importance as an example of an early British scientific research station. It was built in January 1947 by the Falklands Islands Dependencies Survey (FIDS) on the site of the northern base of the 1930s British Graham Land Expedition (BGLE). FIDS had intended to use the BGLE hut which they had checked out the previous year but arrived to find that the hut had been washed away by a tsunami. The men had to return to Port Lockroy and dismantle half of Bransfield House built just three years earlier. Wordie House closed in May 1954 when a new base was established on nearby Galindez Island. Wordie House is managed by the UKAHT and in recent years extensive roofing and flooring works have been carried out to make the building structurally secure and weathertight.

Detaille 66°52'S 66°48'W

Detaille Island Base 'W' (HSM no 83) was used for the purposes of survey, geological and meteorological research along the Loubet Coast. It was occupied for only three winters, being evacuated in March 1959 when sea ice and bad weather made relief by ship impossible. Detaille Island is managed by the UKAHT. In recent years small teams from the Trust have undertaken extensive work to the hut and emergency store to ensure it is structurally secure and weathertight while ensuring it is still apparently unchanged since the men left in 1959. In February 2013, for the first time in 53 years, the postage facility was temporarily re-instated whilst conservation works were carried out.

Horseshoe 67°48'S 67°18'W

Horseshoe Base 'Y' (HSM no 63) on Horseshoe Island in Marguerite Bay, with its outpost Blaiklock Hut, was established in March 1955 to cover the work on the Southern Peninsula, previously carried out from Stonington Base 'E' which had proved difficult to access by ship. However, Horseshoe had its own access problems (survey teams could not easily reach the mainland) and closed in August 1960. The excellent condition and completeness of both the buildings and artefacts are of considerable historical significance; together they provide a very special time-capsule of British life and science in the Antarctic during the late 1950s. There are an estimated 10,000 artefacts on site.

Stonington   68°11′S   67°′00′W

Stonington Base 'E' (HSM no 64) on Stonington Island in Marguerite Bay was established in February 1946 and had two periods of operation from 1946-50 and 1960-75. The famous polar explorer Sir Vivian Fuchs was the base leader in 1948 and 1949. The station closed in 1950 due to continuing difficulties in relief by ship caused by bad sea ice conditions, but reopened again in 1960 when a new hut was erected. The scientific research carried out at the station included topographic survey, geology and meteorology. Base 'E' is adjacent to the US 'East Base' (see below).

East Base   68°11′S   67°′00′W

Stonington Island was chosen as the site for the East Base (HSM no. 55) of the United States Antarctic Service (USAS) Expedition (1939–1941) and named after Stonington, Connecticut, home port of the sloop *Hero* in which Captain Nathaniel Palmer sighted the Antarctic continent in 1820. The base was also home to the Ronne Antarctic Research Expedition 1947-48. East Base is under the care of the US National Science Foundation but with its proximity to Base 'E' (above) whole island management is planned.

The UK Antarctic Heritage Trust Today

Since Port Lockroy was built in 1944 Britain has maintained a continuous presence in Antarctica carrying out survey, scientific research and more latterly, historic building conservation. This solid tradition and the quality of research are second to none. It has generated wide international respect and given the UK a strong, influential position in the affairs of a continent of increasing global importance.

Since 1993 the UK Antarctic Heritage Trust (UKAHT) has grown in influence to become a leading voice on all matters of Britain's Antarctic heritage and is well respected both in the UK and on the international stage. The historic sites on the Antarctic Peninsula are owned by the British Antarctic Survey but under a written agreement the UKAHT cares for and manages them. But it could not do so without its stakeholders and partners:

- The British Antarctic Survey coordinates and conducts Britain's cutting-edge science by operating two permanent research stations at Rothera and Halley and a summer station at Signy. Its work is supported by ships, aircraft, and the Royal Navy.

- The Polar Regions Department of the Foreign and Commonwealth Office administers the political and international aspects of British operations in Antarctica.

- The International Association of Antarctica Tour Operators (IAATO) advocates, promotes and practises safe and environmentally responsible private-sector travel to the Antarctic.

It is visitors to Port Lockroy, in their support of the post office and gift shop, that enable the UKAHT to ensure that the historic buildings continue to be conserved. Beyond that the UKAHT offers assistance (both financial and in-kind) to other polar institutions in the UK and around the world in both outreach and collections conservation and acquisition.

As well as our work to conserve the British historic huts in Antarctica we also run an Oral History Project. The project seeks to collect personal stories and testimonies of those involved in British polar science, with particular focus on those who worked for, or closely with, Operation Tabarin, FIDS and BAS. They offer us a unique and often entertaining insight into the challenges and eccentricities of living in one of the world's most remote environments.

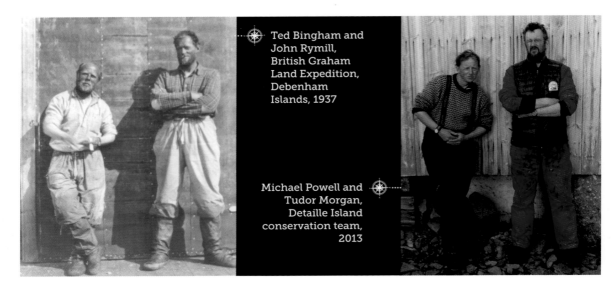

Ted Bingham and John Rymill, British Graham Land Expedition, Debenham Islands, 1937

Michael Powell and Tudor Morgan, Detaille Island conservation team, 2013

Supporting us

Membership makes a difference.

The UK Antarctic Heritage Trust is an independent charity based in the UK that looks after British historic sites on the Antarctic Peninsula. We rely on donations, legacies and the support of visitors to Port Lockroy and our 'Friends of Antarctica' to carry out our vital work.

To find out more or become a 'Friend of Antarctica' visit our website, **www.ukaht.org**

Acknowledgements

The transformation of Port Lockroy and the other Peninsula bases would not have been possible without the support from individuals and institutions far and wide. It is impossible to name them all but for this publication we would like to thank Robert Burton, Alan Carroll, Eleanor Land, Anna Malaos, Rachel Morgan and Tudor Morgan. We could not operate without the support of our key stakeholders and partners: The British Antarctic Survey; The Polar Regions Department of the Foreign and Commonwealth Office; The International Association of Antarctica Tour Operators.

United Kingdom Antarctic Heritage Trust. Charity registered in the UK no. 1024911

The Trust would like to thank those who gave free permission for the use of photographs and pictures:
Helen Annan (33), Sarah Auffret (16), Dominic Barrington (inside page), Florence Barrow (36), Judith Black (37), British Antarctic Survey Archives (11, 12, 16, 17, 21, 23, 26, 27, 29, 30, 31, 33, 34, 41, 47, 48, 49, 50), Geoff Ashley (45), British Antarctic Territory (38, 42), Claire Brown (back cover, 36, 37), David Burkitt (32, 35, 48), Robert Burton Collection (8), Cavalry and Guard Club (10), Alan Cameron (18), Alan Carroll, Wilson Cheung Wai-Yin (2), Jane Cooper (9), John Critchley (14, 24), Peter Gale (7, 9, 10, 11), Graham Gillie (12), John Graham (49), Ylva Grams (12), Edward Hay (5), Rachel Hazell (39), Gordon Howkins (7), Una Hurst (36), Ben Kaye (16), John Killingbeck (51), Florence Kuyper (13, 17, 24), Eleanor Land (19, 20, 17, 24), Paul Leek (18, 20, 22), George Lewis (13, 30), Anna Malaos (52), Nigel McCall (43), Iain McLaughlan (43), Rachel Morgan (3, 8, 10, 13, 20, 23, 26, 37, 41, 46, 51), Tudor Morgan (front cover, 9, 21, 40, 50), Claire Murphy (39, 40), Brian Nixon (28, 35), David Price (27, 31), Rick Price (36), Henry Pollack (47), Michael Powell (38, 39), Russell Family (16), John Smith (28), Scott Polar Research Institute (6, 31, 33, 44, 45, 46, 52), Jon Stephenson (46), Jaap Tinbergen (27), Cat Totty (9, 14, 15, 18, 19, 20, 23, 25), Nigel Watson (43), Fiona Willis (43), Kelly Whybrow (2).

Design and illustrations: www.**artmattersstudio**.co.uk (Bransfield House diagrams, Amy Vale)
Published by the United Kingdom Antarctic Heritage Trust 2014
© United Kingdom Antarctic Heritage Trust